Making Movies

LEVEL 11

DECODABLES BY jump!

Teaching Tips

Lime Level 11

This book focuses on developing reading independence, fluency, and comprehension.

Before Reading

- Ask readers what they think the book will be about based on the title. Have them support their answer.

Read the Book

- Encourage readers to read silently on their own.
- As readers encounter unfamiliar words, ask them to look for context clues to see if they can figure out what the words mean. Encourage them to locate boldfaced words in the glossary and ask questions to clarify the meaning of new vocabulary.
- Allow readers time to absorb the text and think about each chapter.
- Ask readers to write down any questions they have about the book's content.

After Reading

- Ask readers to summarize the book.
- Encourage them to point out anything they did not understand and ask questions.
- Ask readers to review the questions on page 23. Have them go back through the book to find answers. Have them write their answers on a separate sheet of paper.

5357 Penn Avenue South
Minneapolis, MN 55419
www.jumplibrary.com

Decodables by Jump! are published by Jump! Library.

Library of Congress Cataloging-in-Publication Data is available at www.loc.gov or upon request from the publisher.

ISBN: 979-8-88996-948-8 (hardcover)
ISBN: 979-8-88996-949-5 (paperback)
ISBN: 979-8-88996-950-1 (ebook)

Photo Credits

Images are courtesy of Shutterstock.com. With thanks to Getty Images, Thinkstock Photo and iStockphoto. Cover – Prostock-studio. p4–5 – withGod, DC Studio, klyaksun. p6–7 – Sunny studio, Meong Stock Gallery. p8–9 – LI CHAOSHU, vecktor, Mallika Home Studio. p10–11 – Joseph Wright, Photo Oz. p12–13 – Golden Dayz, Gorodenkoff. p14–15 – Motones(Wikimedia), Gorodenkoff. p16–17 – smutny pan, Simbert Brause, Master1305. p18–19 – Iryna Imago, Javier Garcia 65. p20–21 – MIA Studio, wavebreakmedia.

Table of Contents

Making Movies

When you go to the movie theater, you might see a movie about space, dinosaurs, or superheroes. Anything can happen on the big screen! Lots of things that happen in movies could never happen in real life. The people who make movies use lots of amazing technology to make those things look real.

In the last 200 years, there have been many important inventions that have helped make the movies we watch today. In 1896, a French **magician** named Georges Méliès made the first movie. He used camera tricks and **special effects**. Now, almost every movie uses camera tricks and special effects.

Today, most special effects are made using computers.

3D Movies

Most objects are 3D. 3D objects have a height (up and down), a width (side to side), and a depth (forward and backward). However, most photographs and movies are 2D. This means they have a height and width but do not have a depth. Using technology, scientists figured out how to create movies that look 3D.

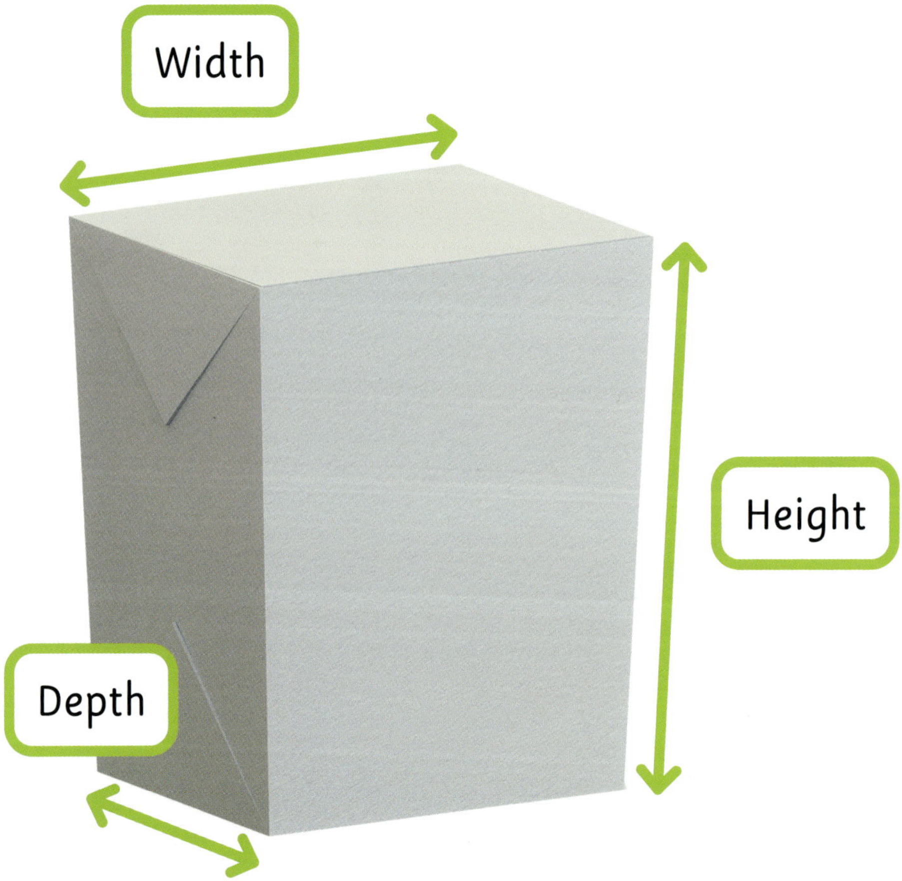

In 3D movies, some objects seem far away, and some seem so close you could touch them. To watch 3D movies, you used to have to wear special 3D glasses. Without these glasses, the screen looked very blurry and confusing. Now, some TVs and theaters have special screens that show 3D movies without needing special glasses.

4D Movies

4D movies use more than sounds and pictures to tell a story. As well as giving us something to see and hear, 4D movies let us use other senses, such as smell and touch. While the story is being told on the screen, things happen to the audience to make it feel more real.

Do you know what the five senses are?

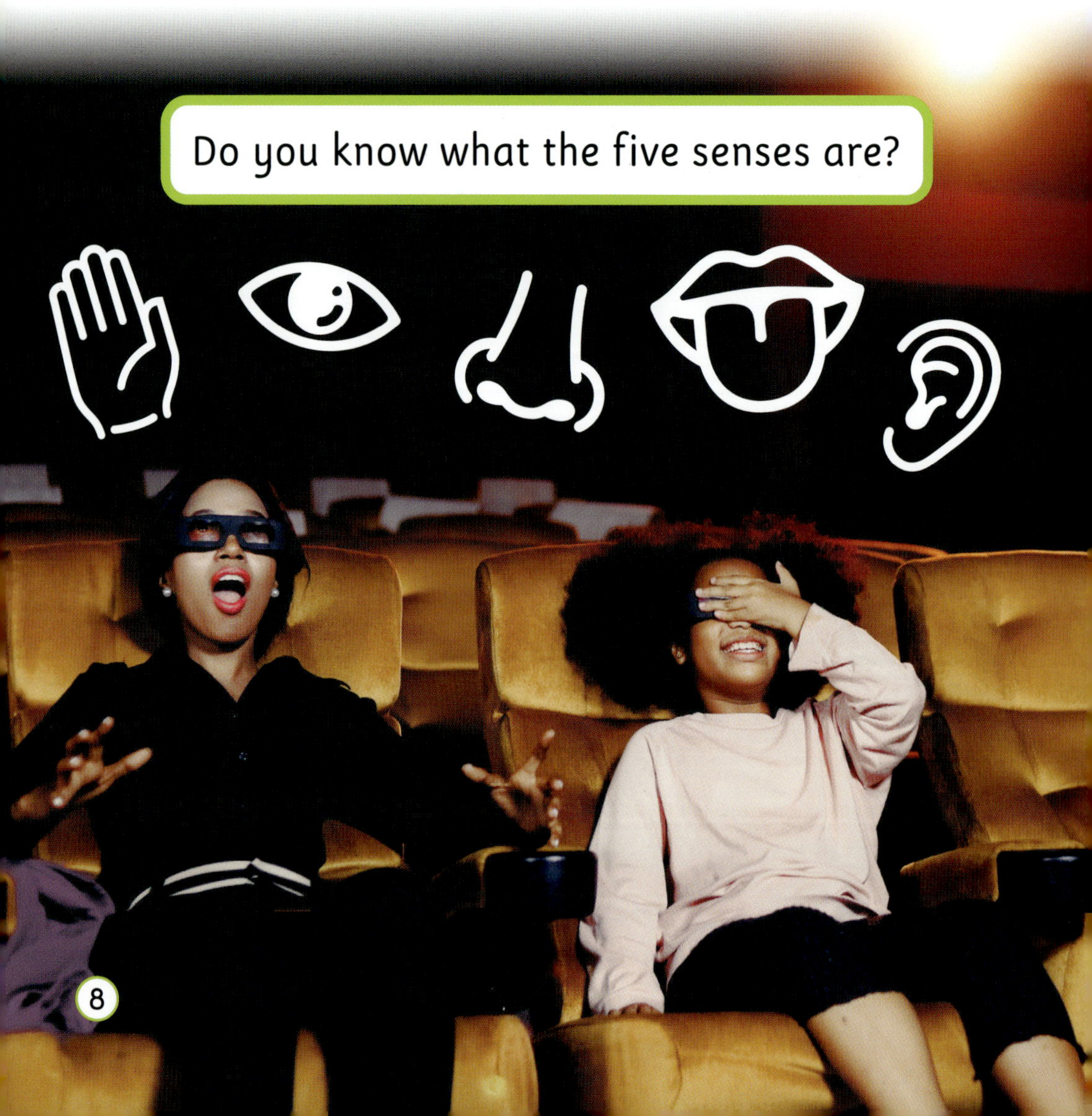

All sorts of special effects are used in 4D movies. If a character falls into a stream, the audience might be splashed with water. If there was something smelly, the theater might be filled with a bad smell. Some people think this will be the future of movie theaters because it creates an experience you cannot get at home.

Animatronics

Animatronics are machines. They are mostly used to create characters and creatures that do not exist, such as dragons or dinosaurs.

Animatronic dinosaur

Today, movies would usually use a technology called **CGI** to create these things. However, sometimes this is not **realistic** enough, especially if something is going to be filmed close-up.

Animatronics can also be useful for actors. Actors are the people who play the different characters in a movie. Animatronics help actors know what the character or creature will look like. Animatronics are usually controlled by remote controls. When a movie is being filmed, there might be someone whose job it is to control the animatronic.

Green Screen

Many impossible things happen in movies. To create these impossible things, movies use CGI. Putting CGI into a scene can be difficult. To make it easier, they use a technology called green screen or chroma keying. Chroma keying works by removing a single shade of color from an image and replacing it with something else.

When moviemakers need to use chroma keying, the scene is often filmed in front of a bright green screen. Green screens are often used to change the background. If a superhero is meant to look like they are flying through the sky, the actor would be filmed lying down or hanging on wires in front of a green screen.

Motion Capture

Motion capture is technology that tracks how a person or object moves in the real world. This movement can then be copied by a CGI character or object. Using motion capture makes the CGI movement look more realistic than if it were all made using a computer.

When filming a scene that uses motion capture, someone acts as the CGI character. However, instead of wearing a costume, the person wears many tiny reflective markers. Once the scene has been filmed, a computer is used to track how and where the markers moved. These movements are mapped onto the CGI character.

Cameras

Cameras are machines that turn light into pictures. They are very important pieces of technology when filming a movie. A camera uses a lens to record an image onto a small piece of tape called a film or onto a computer. Even though movies appear to show moving pictures, cameras can only take one photograph at a time.

To make it look like the picture is moving, the camera takes many photographs very, very quickly. Human eyes can see 20 images a second. If the eye sees more than 20 images a second, the images blur together. Most movies show us 24 images a second, which means the pictures blur together and look like one moving image.

Stop Motion Animation

Stop motion animation is a type of animation. Animation is a way of making still figures look like they are moving. To create stop motion animation, moviemakers put the models into exactly the right position. They take a photograph of the models. Then they move them a tiny bit to put them in the next position.

Most stop motion animation uses 24 photographs per second. This means that for every one second of the movie, the moviemakers had to move each character into 24 different positions. Stop motion animation takes a very long time to make!

Claymation is a popular type of stop motion animation.

The Future of Movies

As new technology is invented, the ways movies are made and watched will change. People used to have to go to the theater whenever they wanted to watch a movie. Now, it is possible to watch movies from home using **streaming sites**. In the future, many movies will not be shown at movie theaters and will only be watched online.

Virtual reality, or VR, is a way of watching movies. VR is a technology that makes you feel like you are inside a virtual world. VR uses a special headset with a screen inside. As you look around and explore, the screen shows you different parts of the virtual world.

Index

How to Use an Index

An index helps us find information in a book. Each word has a set of page numbers. These page numbers are where you can find information about that word.

Page numbers

Example: balloons 5, 8–10, 19

Important word

This means page 8, page 10, and all the pages in between. Here, it means pages 8, 9, and 10.

Questions

1. What special effects might be used in a 4D movie?

2. What is chroma keying also known as?

3. How many images a second can the human eye see?

4. Using the Table of Contents, can you find which page you can read about 3D movies?

5. Using the Index, can you find a page in the book about CGI?

6. Using the Glossary, can you define what streaming sites are?

Glossary

CGI:
Computer-generated images, or images that are made by a computer.

magician:
Someone who performs magic tricks.

realistic:
Very similar to the real thing, or seeming real.

special effects:
Sound or visual effects that are put into movies.

streaming sites:
Online sites that provide media, such as movies, that people can watch.

virtual:
Not actually existing in a physical manner but appearing to do so thanks to technology.